SCRATCHING THE GHOST

SCRATCHING THE GHOST

DEXTER L. BOOTH

Winner of the 2012 Cave Canem Poetry Prize
Selected and Introduced by Major Jackson

GRAYWOLF PRESS

This publication is made possible, in part, by the voters of Minnesota through a Minnesota State Arts Board Operating Support grant, thanks to a legislative appropriation from the arts and cultural heritage fund, and through grants from the National Endowment for the Arts and the Wells Fargo Foundation Minnesota. Significant support has also been provided by Target, the McKnight Foundation, Amazon.com, and other generous contributions from foundations, corporations, and individuals. To these organizations and individuals we offer our heartfelt thanks.

Published by Graywolf Press
250 Third Avenue North, Suite 600
Minneapolis, Minnesota 55401

www.graywolfpress.org

Published in the United States of America

ISBN 978-1-55597-660-6

2 4 6 8 9 7 5 3 1
First Graywolf Printing, 2013

Library of Congress Control Number: 2013939554

Cover design: Kapo Ng @ A-Men Project

Cover art: Margaret Bowland
       White Crows #1, 2007
       Oil on linen, 66 x 56 inches
       © Margaret Bowland, 2007
       Courtesy Driscoll Babcock Galleries, New York

Contents

IV. ABSTRACTS

V. LONG LETTER TO THE 20TH CENTURY

INTRODUCTION

"The life of the consciousness is boundless," so said the Austrian artist Oskar Kokoschka. "It interpenetrates the world and is woven through all its imagery. . . . Therefore we must harken closely to our inner voice. We must strive through the penumbra of words to the core within." Dexter L. Booth's *Scratching the Ghost* makes an argument for poetry marked by a conspicuous imagination nurtured on an intense awareness of one's inner life, the profound mysteries that surround, and the grave threats and hurts that propel such a soul toward a contemplative, expressive art. What is found here: poems of compelling dimensions that go beyond imitative practices and familiar psychological and aesthetic terrain. That boundlessness Kokoschka speaks of threads the remnant of elegance you'll encounter in Booth's poetry, which comes from the old habit of belief in one's lyric self as a testament of one's freedom.

Some will declaim an abhorrence of poetic craft and its features, purporting a façade of dissension, as the young poet I recently read online states: "For a long time, I couldn't understand how people could write in quatrains and still look themselves in the mirror." Others will vocally enunciate its powers and skills in an essentialist act of preserving aesthetic values that are meant to be read as natural law, as in the thinking that iambic pentameter possesses the same rhythm as a human heartbeat. Booth is neither the mercenary nor the rebel; such posturing and demagogy is injurious to

Art. Rather, in reading his poems, one detects a formidable spirit that wants to construct its own horizon of forms, or rather highlight a revealed individuality in refractory utterances that speed headlong toward paradox and enchantment, by any means necessary. Consider the poem "Memory with Fire":

Memory with Fire

Slow burn of time
where our words nudge
into the tiny spaces, reach back,
cower in the corner
of the furthest sound. Of trumpets
and flies. Violins cradled in the hook
of your smile. Again
the smell of the river, warm
as a body beneath me.
The way this moment moves
inside the next.

Or how this piano sits
on its side with our breath
beneath it. Or how you lick
dust from the palm
of your hand to center the wound.
Or how you race beside me
like a stone. Victorious cloud
of bee stings and everything
we should have loved
and didn't.

That the speaker tumbles from each evocative image to that final declaration through a series of sonic concurrences (flies, violins, smile, smell) and musical instrumentation (trumpets, violins, piano) as a means of describing the work of writing, memory, and intimacy, gives you some sense of the lyric sovereignty this poet seeks to claim. Such associative velocity and obliquity is not for the hesitant reader unwilling to release a hunger for prosaic (read: realistic) portrayals of life as though the poem were ordered from an app store. What is thoroughly compelling, equally sensuous, and not at all devoid of emotion, is the authentic mind aiming for understanding ("everything we should have loved / and didn't") in the midst of hidden codes and objects palpitating with, as yet, unperceived meaning. "Memory with Fire" is one of the many poems that could serve as Mr. Booth's ars poetica.

Lest I unwittingly cast Mr. Booth as one among his generation that distrusts continuity, descriptive acts, and narrative edifices, I will direct the reader to his poem "Moon Building," emblematic in that it demonstrates this poet's comfort in deploying a multiplicity of styles. The poem features a speaker who reminisces about a childhood that is "gray and still . . . the way only a child can see it," where a friend's sister instructs that a cracked egg represents a splitting universe, which leads the speaker to see the sun as a yolk (auguring a future life, perhaps, of making similar visual correspondences), which if stared at long enough would endow him with superpowers and an ability to see the future. But, more importantly "the sister's father" appears in this poem (and in subsequent poems), as the anti-hero of the collection:

> I told my sister's father.
>
> He laughed and said:
>
> "If I could eat the sun, imagine what I could do to your mother in bed. Imagine what my palm could do to your ass if I did not have to wait for you to break a branch off that tree in the yard."

and then, later:

> Sometimes it snowed up to our knees and squirrels died in the back yard, frozen in the mouths of hawks. After dinner

we'd wander out, drop our pants and piss our names in the snow.

What we did after that, I can't remember, but I watched my mother through a keyhole once, as she took off her clothes to lie with my sister's father. I should have felt shame. I never built a snowman. When the ice melted we made him a skeleton of twigs and I cried because we could not eat ham or put up a tree. My sister's father said Santa wasn't real, and we didn't have a chimney anyway,

and if someone knocked on our door in a storm, my sister's father would have beaten them like he did my mother, without fear.

The stepfather's violence and presence loom as a counter-force to the speaker's tendency to convey real things under the captivated gaze of the mind's eye while the sensitive spirit of the speaker, even in adulthood looking back, is under siege. The actions of the poem work as allegorical correspondences to the speaker's emotional state. How else to comprehend dead squirrels in the hawk's mouth or peeing one's name in the snow? What is most startling however is the gorgeous juxtaposition of "I should have felt shame. I never built a snowman." The swift correlation of building a snowman as either an antidote to shame or somehow a means by which to open the self to greater feelings, equips the poem with so much ineffable truth. It is such acts of language and intuitive knowledge that gives Mr. Booth his authority and begins to define his unique, lyric self.

Along with Mr. Booth's need to populate his poems with as much of the physical world's concreteness with exactitude and precision, albeit sometimes in the experimental mode, what I find equally charming about *Scratching the Ghost* is his effort to transmute so much autobiographical material into the realm of art, as though he sought to dispassionately replenish the self inside his poems. Sometimes this occurs through the most conventionally anecdotal means by which we come to expect from personal narratives. And yet, notice how the speaker remains unruffled on the surface of the poems, then detect all the enormous feelings bubbling underneath: regret, anger, suffering, guilt, gratitude—it's all there, but mostly insinuated, which is a masterful display of restraint, tension, and unwavering desire to make one's journey known.

In Favor of Company

> I barely knew her then. We sat on a bench sharing a
>   Parliament
> and an awful postcard view of rocks polka dotted with
>   pigeon shit,
> old train tracks like a monolithic machine left
> to watch over the edge of the earth, water so dark beneath
> its shadow that it hurt to look into. It was hot that day
> and the ground was bare with the stubble of grass
> hanging over the pathway like frat boys on balconies
> puking out their guts before dawn.

The way the poems gift the reader with memorable images, and yet also conceal any triggering narrative, while also teeming subterraneously with emotions makes for a unique experience with language and paradoxically allows a reader to substitute or inhabit even more the absent, yet attendant emotions that arise with each image, such as "frat boys on balconies" and "stubble of grass" over pathways. At times, Mr. Booth gives the impression that he is not in control; however, this is an illusion.

The above poem, like so many others in the collection, reveals, in fact, that a greater, deliberate composing mind is at work in this book, which with each reading earns my profoundest admiration and reignites my belief in poetry to embody the consciousness of those who can tinker language to a ritual of magic and awe.

Major Jackson

SCRATCHING THE GHOST

I said to my soul, be still, and wait without hope
For hope would be hope for the wrong thing; wait without love
For love would be love of the wrong thing; there is yet faith
But the faith and the love and the hope are all in the waiting.
Wait without thought, for you are not ready for thought:
So the darkness shall be the light, and the stillness the dancing.

—T. S. Eliot, "East Coker"

I. Meditations on Self-Crucifixion

Meditations on Self-Crucifixion

When I die, beneath what will be
left, the crust of Wednesday,
be faithful to the cuts and carpet burns,
scent of my feet. Forget the toaster,
the way the wire swings, my wrist
in waving. Thin mist of blue
mosquitoes. Wings tucked in,
secret islands.

Better for the target
lipsticked on the bathroom mirror.
Soap carved into sandals
laid by the open window.

x x x

Husk of coconut,
sweet breath of the fig,
what remains? Caught
in the tile and shallowed
beach-mud. Water stains
and shower bells. Sound
of the leaky throat.
The hand that made everything

sing. Forgive

me. I have not
yet found the sand for bathing.

If there is light, we move
in its sternum. How wild,
the human need

for weakness. Stay close
to the walls, the hunger
grasping at your legs: to be
the final, open gate.

II. Little Myths Initiated by Rain

Memory with Water

If there is weight to your words
that explains the bowing.
Briefly the center of gravity circles
your head with the sickness of wolves.

Where there are lemons, we shy away
from the small talk of fingers,
the intimacy of fire at rest,

zest or blood. To be clear,

I envy little boys
that jacket   your world.
When you move, they fall
to the corners of your brain,
your cheeks. In white
overalls they become teeth,
and they know well the damp soil
of your gums: thickness of your tongue
like the severed tail of a monster   that curls
in the citrus bile of fable,

reverse   blooms in the mouth
of a rose. Threatened
reflection of the lotus
    heavy with the damp touch of night,
please take us away. Please
take us   away.

Anniversary

—for my mother

She puts on her wig like a smile
thrown sideways with the tilt of a little child's head.
I watch her adjust it like an expression
or a tie, the temperature in a freezing room.

Inside she is worn
like the pages of my favorite books,
her teeth yellowing at the edges of each word,
lips turned down in the corners.
Her eyeliner highlights
my favorite lines in black, and I am
reading her face with open palms,
squinted eyes,

my whole life changing
down the sides of her face, the future
pooling on the floor.

Self-Elegy as River

Blue pipe cleaners, tape, empty vodka bottles.
(Say *water.*)

Sister by the window with an afro, purple
tongue, swollen jaw. It happens this way. Wisdom
teeth uprooted like heavy summer
guiding smells from the river
where this little boat can carry silence

(Lego blocks. Rubber cement.)
            around the neck that processes
            air like an equation.

x x x

A decade later you are still riding my first bike,
too large to move beyond the porch,
bare feet tethered to the training wheels
with fishing wire.

You are lost. At sundown
the doors creak shut: weathered fist.

x x x

And will death be like rolling over during sleep?
Apnea—the mythology of the slipping tongue.

Once you won a bet by licking a wooden cross
on Christmas day (but please don't tell
that story again. We all know how it should have ended)
and it began to snow (they said *just after*)
            you put your lips around Jesus' palm.

You did admit to being holy
      (Why holy?)
Now that tongue rolls
      behind the teeth.
         The only thing you could ever keep to yourself.
            Little wrecking ball.
            Tiny muscle of demise.

In Favor of Company

I barely knew her then. We sat on a bench sharing a Parliament
and an awful postcard view of rocks polka dotted with pigeon shit,
old train tracks like a monolithic machine left
to watch over the edge of the earth, water so dark beneath
its shadow that it hurt to look into. It was hot that day
and the ground was bare with the stubble of grass
hanging over the pathway like frat boys on balconies
puking out their guts before dawn.

Only Skin

On a walk near the train tracks we found a condom,
empty and broken, and she took my silence
        to mean something.
We wound up by the river and I thought,
        little myths initiated by rain.
                Always fear,

even of the young who move
        across the silver back of the water
where three girls jump Double Dutch.
She held that cigarette as though it could save her
from tragic news—
        flies buzzing loudest before the passing of a friend—
and we listened for the broken-throated hymn of rope on pavement.
She told me that death is not the end of the story,
and I believed her because she was dying, and died alone.

Moon Building

I can't remember her name, but I remember being four, her hands cradling my hips like the small planet that I was, perched on the edge of the sink, feet curled like talons. I watched her boyfriend through the window, shoveling snow from the lawn onto the windshield of the car she had barely been able to start to get us there.

She asked when I needed to be home, but I could not remember.

The world was gray and still then, the way only a child can see it. I was invincible under the blankets of joy and curiosity. There was no separation between the ground and the sky, and her boyfriend could have easily been lifted and devoured by the frost-glare of her eyes. I still can't remember

the color of the scarf she gave me when she sent me out for the mail and whispered,
    "Just breathe through your nose, sweetie,"

or the color of my socks, thick and darkening with snow, or my shorts she unbuttoned with two soapy and shivering fingers—

her saying, "Go ahead, Dexter, pull out your jimmy. Piss on every plate and spoon," and me doing it, convinced everything I gave was precious.

When the wind picked up I saw him beating the hood with the shovel. I saw her polishing that plate, food stuck to it like gum, and it was like the time in kindergarten I asked about time travel, and Mrs. Slaughter told me not to worry.

That evening Jerry's sister said that every time she cracked an egg, our universe was splitting; every dimension existed in a shell. The yolk, of course was the sun we stared at two hours a day to see the future and gain super powers—resulting in vomiting and glasses for us both. I told my sister's father.

He laughed and said:

"If I could eat the sun, imagine what I could do to your mother in bed. Imagine what my palm could do to your ass if I did not have to wait for you to break a branch off that tree in the yard."

We were forbidden to go beyond that tree but, unsupervised we wandered into the Indian graveyard behind our houses, climbed the totems—which were later knocked down and stripped to make room for condos. When it snowed my mother came home with bags of Christmas gifts from the church, bags of water guns, decks of cards and press-on tattoos.

Sometimes it snowed up to our knees and squirrels died in the back yard, frozen in the mouths of hawks. After dinner we'd wander out, drop our pants and piss our names in the snow.

What we did after that, I can't remember, but I watched my mother through a keyhole once, as she took off her clothes to lie with my sister's father. I should have felt shame. I never built a snowman. When the ice melted we made him a skeleton of twigs and I cried because we could not eat ham or put up a tree. My sister's father said Santa wasn't real, and we didn't have a chimney anyway,

and if someone knocked on our door in a storm, my sister's father would have beaten them like he did my mother, without fear.

Anyway, I am wiping my feet on the doormat of memory, thinking maybe one day my sister will remember when we caught an ant and a bee in a mason jar just to see who would survive. If the bee won, I would have to set it free. If the ant won, I would have to eat it. If they both died we would fill the jar with water, wait days for it to cloud like the sky—knowing that aging was worse than this death we were giving—sediment of arms and wings.

Waste

1.

In fifth grade, I might have pissed myself because Ms. Jackson said I could not leave, because we were testing and I might sneak out to a friend and borrow their book. Maybe I might have sat with my legs crossed, waiting for the bell to ring, tapped my foot against the chair of the girl in front of me until she thought I was flirting, and smiled. I might have pissed myself. I might have been the last kid to the bus, lying and telling the boys in the back *a sprinkler went off under my crotch.* Maybe I said, *that smell is from Jerry in Science class. He doesn't bathe. He farted on my leg.* And maybe that's the truth.

2.

At the Children's Museum my job was to help dress and undress Barney, the purple dinosaur. Inside his suit the guy said he felt like Robocop, with his voice modifier and overhead fans. It was hard to dance, he said, standing on platforms, and when I unzipped his back he slid out like a retroverted fetus. A boy lost on his way from the bathroom had his face pressed to the window. He said, *I didn't know Barney had human guts* and I said, *neither did I.*

3.

Field Day, the school purchased an old car from the scrap yard. Ten tickets gave you five minutes to whack it with a sledgehammer, as if you were playing whack-a-mole. Between the two of us, David and I destroyed the windows, caved in the trunk and bent the hubcaps from the tires. They gave us the muffler for an extra three tickets when we got bored. We were ten. We would have given everything away for someone to tell us we were men.

The Body

They split the hog down the middle.

It was cold and raining, I remember
the steam and the knife and the squeal and how

they all left the body like a ghost.
They lasted and lasted and the body shook
in your hands. I was
told *this is sex my friend,*

       be still.

× × ×

Take care to roll it
like a swollen log
pushed up from the belly
of the river. Gently turning
it over, take note of the red
ants harvesting what is left
beneath the bark.

Be gentle. It might all just fall apart at your touch.

× × ×

But I know little of the shape of a breast,
perhaps that it curves like a spoon on the tongue.
Your mother had one breast.
I touched it
once. It was a dare

and I was promised
it was the only way
to become a man.

No one thought to call the police.

They ran when she began coughing
up blood. I opened her shirt,
pushed on her nipple like an alarm.

x x x

It was the time
your sister danced up
and down the aisles in church.
She was possessed
by some ghost,
a beast built like your father.

We sang.

There was dinner:
        white bread and someone's blood.
They dipped her in the water

and your father said she was clean.

Short Letter as Incantation

If I do not address you, know I did not forget your name. The letters are still arranged the way they fell. I see your eyelids folding over the world, how terrible it must be, for only seconds at a time, to see everything so beautifully wrapped in its dark skin: nights we might have spent at the window, naming all the stars you know . . .

Under the Weather

1.

A child once told me the sun is the deadliest animal—
violent, never blinking. On Sundays
I sit on this mountain with a bottle of water and a book—
any book—not reading, jotting balloons in the margins.

I don't go outside enough, and I know it, imagine
the landscape circling my window at night,
mountains angry and foaming with weather.

There are reasons I sleep until noon,
Ignore the hours, patchy and corn-yellow on my eyelids.

Up north they say the hills move slowly like tongues . . .

✕ ✕ ✕

I saw a video once of people gathering to burn
letters to loved ones who had passed.
They were sick with grief, but shuffled around the fire
waiting for someone to speak.

I once heard you whisper
        The decision to give words to suffering
        is still a decision.

2.

A man robbed a Walmart in Ohio.
When the cops were called he ran and hid
in a dumpster. The not-so-funny part is that he was
picked up by a truck and compacted
for an hour. He called 911 from the truck, screaming
that he was being crushed, that he couldn't feel his legs.

It took the cops another hour to pinpoint the truck
and they tried but couldn't pull him out. They dumped
him on the street and said all they could see was an arm,
dangling from a mound of flattened boxes.

I only laughed because of how easily it could have been me.

3.
Dear pomegranate,
dear wild iris and seed, I will do things differently the first time—
     again.

× × ×

Before I peel the curtains back like flaps of skin,
what I am rolls over in the body,
restless—the window chattering,
          the voice of a truck moving through everything
               like a ghost.

I fear the news the way I fear the truth.

On the mountain the sweat coats my face
like pollen. The higher I go the more anxious
I become. My heart is swollen as a calf
bitten by a spider, the body
dragging itself in delirium, going everywhere
but home.

III. Our Famous Shadows

Memory with Fire

Slow burn of time
where our words nudge
into the tiny spaces, reach back,
cower in the corner
of the furthest sound. Of trumpets
and flies. Violins cradled in the hook
of your smile. Again
the smell of the river, warm
as a body beneath me.
The way this moment moves
inside the next.

Or how this piano sits
on its side with our breath
beneath it. Or how you lick
dust from the palm
of your hand to center the wound.
Or how you race beside me
like a stone. Victorious cloud
of bee stings and everything
we should have loved
and didn't.

Scratching the Ghost

—for Granny

Tonight, you are bald, your head dented
like the moon. There are no faces
just the cold, cheesy yellow reflected
from the ceiling. We are gray.
The night embraces us. Pulls us
so close we can smell its musk
and cologne. Still,

the clouds offer their somber news
through cracks in the blinds.
Their splayed fingers are dancing
in tune to Kenny G. The stub of your left leg dangles
as I hold you up, my hands under your arms
like a child. You are complaining about the itch,
the burn; scratch the ghost of your calf and heel.

If I could, I would massage your age away,
push back the wrinkles with some child's
grim reaper mask. You can be a little girl forever
if you want. Put on your glasses, I'll spin you some more.
We'll pretend that dawn isn't knocking.
I'll turn up the music, switch off the porch lights.
We'll dance like there's nobody home.

Letter to a Friend

—for Danielle

I always come back to these woods
    feeling guilty under the accusing
leaves. How everything changes—
    a mother again loses her son to the stream.

But who documents the fire? In our language
    there are seven words that mean *hope.*
Little girls dance here in Winter,
    follow their circled steps into Spring.

This was the poem I wrote you on the week drive from Virginia to
Arizona, scribbling lines on my arm at rest stops. Driving at dawn
you begin to think the world is winking at you, the low lights of the
city replaced by hills. I had never seen so much earth, and being
alone, had never felt so much like dust, but I rose in the morning
because that's what I thought of: being human.

Next to dying and masturbation there is not much one does well
alone. In each motel I measured my legs and tried to calculate the
weight of my brain because I read that if a human is blindfolded
and asked to walk in a straight line we will always go in circles, no
matter how we try.

At night I made diagrams and marked the map, wrote:

"Mud remembers the closing cocoon of snow,
    changing arithmetic of wind."

I'm still not sure what it means. One night I dreamt of driving in a
fog so thick I couldn't see my hands. I kept passing my house. No
matter what exit I took there it was, my sister and mother ghost-
shadowed on the porch. You were never there. I might have called
you in a dream, to tell you some celebrity had died; cardiac arrest
the news said, while I stopped breathing.

Your mother probably told you I wasn't trying hard enough to move forward, but now when I look back all I can see is that empty bed. When I wake your voice crackles in my head like a short-wave radio. All I can hear is *I'm sorry. It'll never happen again.*

My Favorite Mistakes

1.
On a Friday night I find myself
drinking and alone, pacing the house
where your grandmother used to live.
The house is condemned now,
the windows gutted and boarded up.
The grass high enough
to hide me when I sneak in
through the back.

With your daughter's pink chalk
I scribble your name
on every wall. Mark out the spaces
where all your furniture used to be.
Then I sit in the living room, playing
air guitar until morning.

2.
When the maggots were done
with the owl, we built a city
with its bones and populated it
with Lego men, bottle caps and
cotton. We gave them
telescopes and guns
and once a month faked meteor showers.
We were gods,
so we built them
a plastic church where they could pray.

Prayer at 3 a.m.

I washed your father's pants in the kitchen sink.
That should have been enough to tell you
I am still convinced there is no difference
between kneeling and falling if you don't get up.

The head goes down in defeat, but lower in prayer,
and your sister tells me each visit that she has learned
of a new use for her hands.

I've seen this from you both: cartwheels through the field
at dawn, toes popping above the corn stalks like fleas
over the heads of lepers. Your scarecrow reminds me

of Jesus, his guilt confused for fear.
The sun doesn't know; the fog lifts
everything in praise.

This Side Up

On cold nights we huddled against the warm light of a computer screen, watching viral videos of mining accidents and cave detonations. It was best on mute, the dark socket of the cave lit up and handled by gravity. How strange, for a second, to witness the ground meeting the sky, the sky that foams like the ocean.

. . .

At the park people walk their dogs and you ask me again why we can't bring the cat on a leash. There are college students playing basketball, some off drinking or smoking pot under a tree. I laugh. Everything is genetic, including laziness, they say, and I think of this as I watch two girls hanging upside down from the monkey bars, their dresses settling over their heads like clouds.

. . .

Your sister's fish swam upside down for three days before it died. A broken swim bladder makes for six days of crying and two of observational fun. She asked me about it and I said all fish go to heaven, and the fish was always swimming in the right direction from birth—we only see it this way because our brain processes what the eye really wants—the ascension, and seeing the world as you go.

Letter of Self-Abduction

It is all I can do to urge this breath, this child I have blindfolded
and led by candy into the forest. Here, what I eat is only recognizable
by touch, slick feathers of memory; reflective,
heavy and damp.

To be truthful, I crawled on my belly until I was twenty.
I broke my nose violently kissing feet. What else could I have been
looking for but passage? For the lips to probe for something more
to witness than the body I praise, even as it fails?
I smell what is sweet now, and softly knotted
in surrender. Still, I wished these thorns, crooked and stained,
I wished this flayed skin above the brow to accept
their committed bending. What is taken from me belongs
where it lands when it slips finally through; this echo,
our curious warning, the kindling ravaging my ankles
like dogs, as though nothing is precious to this land
but the sheltering dread.

Fire

When my grandmother died my sister's father wore a purple suit to the funeral. He rode on a red Harley at the head of the procession, like a single berry floating on the shoulders of a dark stream. My mother cried for many reasons that morning. My sister's father said he'd break the limousine driver's face for trying to feel her up while she was in grief. Really he was helping her to the car because she couldn't stand, because the car was an invitation to see my grandmother's body. Still, they bought her wheelchair and set it open and empty at the end of the pew, like they expected her to climb out of the coffin and raise her hands in praise. My sister's father said we could move in with him again. Because he was not like us he wouldn't sing or pray for my grandmother's soul. She hated him, and when the light shone just right through the stained glass windows, I thought I saw his jacket smoking, thought I saw a bead of sweat, like an inchworm, making for the leaf of his collar.

No Ark or Landing

And my son, who will build
fences made of toothpicks,
a grape atop each one, he will say
"father, ahead."

x x x

So, to that time
we gave each other Bic tattoos.
When you pressed as hard as you could
until the faintest traces of cheap ink held to my skin.
The mustache I gave you was really just two sideways
trees. Because you could think of nothing more you wrote:

My father.
My father.

x x x

We could not lower our heads
from the clouds, from the joke we made
of eating them, growing fat and light. Of you
eating them. Growing
fat. And light . . .

x x x

This is

the predictable image of me at seven,
my hand dipped in red tempera paint,

the first creation, the first
conception of an idea; of white paper
    holding my first identity,
            something like a strawberry
                        in the snow.

x x x

As in the unpredictable nebulae of lips,
which has everything to do with our hands.
How they learned to draw
stick figures on the flattened skin
of a toilet paper roll. How they cut them out with shakes
  took away little parts
    of a head, a forearm,
or the ankle
 that we said later was a foot,
or even later was an open mouth
        we painted red with a tube of lip gloss.

How they took away the parts of ourselves
we were not happy with,
    as if they knew we wanted more than to be

    a circle, for a moment. A head
without a body. A continuation of what
is left behind. What is used until it can be
used no more.

x x x

But does it all go back to grease? To creating things
just to name them? To understand
we built a wall of snowballs packed in foil,

only stood to watch them fly into the eye
of the window. Only to watch our youth give way to glass;
an inversion of everything we had
grown to be.

Piano . . . bookshelf . . .

. . . sometimes we name things as a way of counting the years . . .

mirror . . . picture frame . . . vase.

Short Letter to the 20th Century

Sometimes it's a Bugs Bunny candle; gloves clutching dynamite like a sword. No, what I wished for was colorful and small, like lies. Two bendy straws, blue plastic for the spot I couldn't reach and shouldn't scratch in front of strangers. Maybe that girl I liked was there. She ripped filters off her grandmother's cigarettes. Her foot fell asleep, or I did, on the couch with one eye open. My mother is singing. I apologize: this should never have happened at all.

Our Famous Shadows

This ends like a fable,
    deep in the throat of woods
where the trees have threaded the sky
a subtle ochre and green

by noon.

Every voice is a moving body.
    Squirrels hustle to bury their spoils.
Moss barnacles the hills.

Here is what I have given: prayer,
    for once; another type of song.

Perhaps we have all taken long walks past churches
    and whispered for salvation
from the threatening doom call of a bell.

I had friends once, but I was young.

The three of us stopped so Ekow could shit
in the bathroom next to the altar.
The church was as desolate and endless
    as dreamless sleep.

"Thank you, dear Lord..." he said
and I thought, *this is what death smells like.*

Being Catholic, David might have actually
been praying, his tongue moving
    even before the priest rushed us out
into the garden—the three of us,
young and frail as wafers—the priest saying,

"I want your names.
    I am going to tell your father."

David lied,
Ekow gave the priest his real name and address,
and I said I did not know my father, which is still true.

We left as it grew dark,
          as the world prepared to take from us again.

x x x

I awaken from a dream, settling back into the body
    the way soil amends after rain.
 I have not given much else. My thoughts,
perhaps, the sounds of what I carry inside. I have given
    fear, I remember. I might have given compassion.

There were years I would not step on ants
    or swat a fly. Where the structure of nature depended
        on the song arranged and reassembled by the flapping
            of a wing.

And something still tolls in my bones.
Something has followed me here.

x x x

In third grade Dominique Joyner chased me
    out of history class. We cut down the stairs
and I touched every squared corner
    of the chain-linked playground fence. I lost a shoe
and it gleamed suddenly behind me,
    a useless hole in my life.

So, I have given memory.
I have given memory and a shoe.

IV. Abstracts

Abstract # 1

The wind has crushed us,
our bone-dust dumped
into the night like stars.

Abstract #2

So many crows dead
on the ground, the night
refuses to rise, for fear
its face may break
away in flight.

Abstract #3

Mouths foaming

like a scar after
the sweet kiss
of peroxide.

Tails like rice.
Cotton eyes.

There is not enough light
in the clouds to hide
the smell. White deer
lying in the streets like sand.

Abstract #4

Corpses we call
heroes. Bones we venerate
with names. Cover them
in the dirt of our fables,
rock-mist of our myths,

to be picked at by the worms
of difference they cannot see.
Paper boats of change
folded before death
to voyage blind,
with good fortune in the rain.

Abstract #5

god
flesh

thin pulp
of paper
pressed
and kneaded
by the cold
fingers

of children

steaming milk
spotted on pants
like urine

drink in the day
through an open mouth
psalm

Abstract #6

our david

dreams of giants too tiny
to hide like pins
in the hem of your dress
grateful fondling of fingers
large boulders
collapsing
like a mine
on the city
where we slept

rocking gently
in the wind
like a sling

Abstract #7

If it comes, let it come
like twin moons
in the night,
split the skin from the darkness,
climb out like mirrored mornings.

x x x

If it comes, let it
come softly
like the rubbing of wings,
skeleton for tinder.
Song from flint.

x x x

If it comes, let
it come like
silence. Lumbering mountain,
treacherous trail
of light.

x x x

If it comes,
let it come
quickly, be
an arm stretched
from the sun,
star soot under
your nail,
when you touch me,
up from the dead.

x x x

If it
comes, let it
come running
like the teeth of chainsaws,
with noise and quiet flame;
as when angels kiss humans
in the presence of the tree.

✘ ✘ ✘

If
it comes, let it
come from me,
from the fondness
of my hands,
laid over pallets and bones
piecing together
what remains
                without skin.

V. Long Letter to the 20th Century

Memory with Silence

Believe the clouds, the web of bones they carry
in announcement. Winter wrapped
in the vice of stinted labels. Yellow is the dust

that saves. Yellow malt and fibers,
rice capsules of glass and steel,
hanging beads of water and mountain:

envy of the sky. How geometric,

here, the shape of space.
Wires returning to god-head,

totem of desire, gouged
center of time, door hinge of the leaf set.

× × ×

Forget the giant's foot. Announce the heroes
dipped in wine. The names of martyrs
given compensation in bread
for what it is to remember.

So far, the mildew and lint. The unfaithful
laws of moving. Seed
of the radish. Destruction
of chalk as a city under siege.

× × ×

Broken trumpet,
the age you announce is fleeting,

Flock of sparrows, your wingtips
give quiet solace to the evening.

Set fire to the bushel,
your birthdays lined up and twined,
named for the book or chapter.

Glass tongue, vengeful letters:
we assembled you
for the safety of weather
on the palm, sweat-rivers
on the pillow.

Letter to a Five-Year-Old

Gus said to me, *you gotta teach those fuckers who's boss. None of that floppin' around and shit—have a club ready, or a mallet, and just catch 'em a few times right in the face. Gotta let 'em know they're gonna be dinner, fuckin' fish, unless they're little. Then they get lucky and you put the son of a bitch back in the water and wait till next Spring.* This reminded me of your song—cloud missiles and trout librarians, the smell of scale-cut hands and raw, glue-peeled fingers; the evening we waited for your mother to pick you up, the sky bruising over like fruit.

You drew on napkins because your mother couldn't afford paper, closed your eyes and made overlapping circles, whispered, "Life." I taught you songs about potatoes and spaghetti, taught you colors until you forgot I kept your napkin because you said "You're my friend," and "how will you find me in the dark?" pointing out the museum window to where I told you your mother was lost, circling a fern to find you.

Sure, you were right. That thing you said about the trees—that the leaves and the trunk are two separate animals, like humans, co-dependent—attached at the bone. Even now I remember how your sister never left your side, how she wouldn't look at me, spoke into your shoulder, and you translated: "Thank you for the crayons." What else was there to say? I heard sirens everyday in the city. On this muffled desert night I imagine them finding your mother, how rumors spread of her careening like a vulture around the block, thirty miles away, searching for a crack den.

There is magic in forgiveness. Gus was only half-joking about the fish, but I've looked into the eyes of a guppy many times, dangling, mouth-snared from a string. They are your eyes, coin-round and desperate as I walked you to the officers, explained that not all people were good, but they would take care of you.

I still have your napkin. Often I look at it and wonder if you remember the lyrics to that song. Trout librarian. Missile Cloud. . . . *then they get lucky . . . back in the water . . . wait till Spring.*

Ars Poetica with Silence and Movement

1.
There is nothing to write about decay:
dust settles on everything.
This poem will become a paper crane
nestled amongst others in the clay
cup my sister made me. Sage betrays
my fear of storms, waters the eyes that strain
against morning light. If it rains
there will be plenty to write about today—

the smell of bodies on wet sheets like
larvae, newly hatched in the sternum
of a bird. Stone fruit overripe,
darkly bruised. Clouds leave their phantoms
in mud and sand, weighted leaves strike
the roof of my body in a piercing tantrum.

2.
The roof of my body in a piercing tantrum,
divides my thoughts—the way land splits open
to smile or frown at what is stolen by the ocean.
This headache becomes a reminder of why I seldom
equate weather with love. I succumb
to tracing bolts of lightening and broken
patterns in time carried away, swollen
        in the bubble of memory, flash tandem

to sound. Everything feels painfully unending
at the close of day—the horizon raw
with the squall of birds, your singing rends
everything feathered from the sky; claws
tapping the counter far away, blending
with the synchronized movement of your jaw.

3.

With the synchronized movement of your jaw—
windows opened like veins, headlights dusting
this memory—the glow of time continues rusting
my ribcage until nothing can move, withdrawing
the clockwise spin of marrow, the flesh that thaws
to let life in.

       My sister began adjusting
         to her body. At eighteen she's trusting
my opinion on boys, no longer drinking with straws.
Yes, I visited home.
       My mother's losing
her hair. My sister says the new wig looks
like a dog. My friends ask if I'm schmoozing
with famous writers. I don't even have a chapbook.
They don't know what chapbook means, refusing
me in their jealousy, tongues curved like hooks.

4.

In their jealousy, with tongues curved like hooks,
my friends become large shadowy figures of air.
       We're not your people anymore. Tear
       the skin from your bones, let the hungry
       out west use the sun to bleach and cook
       your tongue. You are alone.

                             I feel impaired
by metaphors for loneliness, aware
that when I left my home, the city shook,
the streets a mantle of voices, gathering dust.

There is always plenty to write about decay:
my sister's father has gout, his leg is pus,
swelling skin. He has the will to pray,
believes there is still power in words—he must.
       Cigarettes in the cup, cranes in the ashtray.

5.

Cigarettes in the cup, cranes in the ashtray,
a break to recall secrets admitted in anger:
　　　for years I have considered everyone a stranger,
　　　willing to concede, everyday like doomsday,
　　　things crumbling around me.
　　　　　　　　　I hit replay
　　　　　　　　　　　　　after taking a nap, list the dangers
　　　　　　　　　　　　　living in my head, the hollow
　　　　　　　　　　　　　　　chambers
　　　　　　　　　　　　　　　　endlessly stretched and
　　　　　　　　　　　　　　　　　divided like a highway

　　　　　　　　　　　　　that curls back on itself.
　　　　　　　　　　　　　This is life,

　　　　　　　　　　　　rain, the smell of bodies on
　　　　　　　　　　　　　　wet sheets,
　　　　　　　　　　the slit in the blinds that lets in a
　　　　　　　　　　　　blade of light—
　　　　　　　　　　creation of a memory that repeats:
　　　　　　　friends, we protected the dying
　　birds with a butter knife.
Remember? Oh, youth, even now the song retreats.

6.

Remember youth? Even now the song retreats
back down my throat, catching like
hair, like veins that move, not eternal
as sand. I no longer suffer self-deceit.

　　　The moon swings through the trees like a ball of concrete
　　　and I commit to the freedom of being nocturnal,
　　　to speak to the night as though it were a journal
　　　to which I admit my fears, in which I mistreat

　　　my past incarnations as a silly child without
super powers—no x-ray vision, no cape,

no sense of the future or the shootout
behind my skull. Another piece of tape
to hold together the body during a drought,
as the cicada thrum follows me across this landscape.

7.
As the cicada thrum follows me across this landscape
 I hear a congregation of voices trying to assert
 the past. Everything that moves brings comfort
 now, the cycle of progression: the cranes become snowflakes,

my shoelace a horizon that holds everything in balance, intimate,
endearing. The flesh thaws again, alert
  with life, the cells in concert, as a birch
that vibrates with sparrows. I no longer ache to duplicate

rainy mornings, to let last year generate the future.

        Note to lovers and friends who have spurned and betrayed:
the language we used to share is so peculiar
 now. I suture the divide, move on to survey
the grounds for intruders—I swear tomorrow will be smoother.
There will be nothing to write about that day.

Queen Elizabeth

John, you asked me what it was like to be black,
to come from a place where being black mattered.

I thought of telling you that being black matters
everywhere. Your great-grandfather owned this land,
the dust and the Gila Monsters, cattle prods and mountain ranges.

I wondered if your family owned slaves.

x x x

In Ethiopia, they practice scarification because the skin is too dark
for tattoos. Women are whipped and it is consensual.
The body bleeds and swells; this is bravery. For a boy to become
    a man
he must jump over a herd of cattle. He is marriageable
only after his sisters are lashed, because this is the bond of skin—
        this is letting go.

x x x

Where I come from, Jesus is dark-skinned and forgiving.
My mother has seen him. My sister does not care.

Your father was a minister, and I am curious to know,
if the Son of the desert is also the Son of the city,
and if so, why is there still so much hatred between them?

At the bar, after a poetry reading, some kid said,
    I don't want to be a black writer.

I thought of slugging him with the nearest bottle;
his skin was darker than my own.
An hour before, a friend of his read a poem

in dialect to a packed crowd. She was a homeless man
begging for God's forgiveness.

(*Lawd, I ain't got nowhere else to go*)

This girl needed my approval, asked if I was offended.
       I have thought before,
       I don't want to be a black writer.

   ✳ ✳ ✳

When I got into grad school my uncle said,
"You're goin' out there to try n'be smart,
like the white people."

The only girl I ever dated that my mother liked
was from New York. She said to me once
she only liked white men.
We discussed it at a party and someone asked,
"Then why are you two together?"

Now I think the answer is simple, though I'm no longer
sure of the question: Anthropologists say
there are fewer UV rays in the northern hemisphere,
more below the equator.

That might explain everything.

Like how, in Kenya, women are so desperate
to be perfect that they cover their faces with
skin lighteners made from mercury,
lotions with names like "Queen Elizabeth"
and "Body Clear," knowing that they are illegal,
lead to organ failure, and death.

When my sister calls again I will tell her,
       You are beautiful.

Miss Harrison's Fifth Grade Project

Great Uncle Irvin had no words. Of thirteen children he is the last, and at times he forgets himself, says he spoke to my grandmother last night. Two months ago he drove shirtless at midnight to visit his daughter, and when he couldn't remember why he left the house, he pulled off the Interstate, sat terrified in a mall parking lot. For a night he was Cecelia, who suffered terribly from Alzheimer's and slowly lost the ability to remember, speak, then swallow. When the officer knocked on his window and asked where he was headed, great uncle Irvine couldn't remember. Great uncle Irvin had no words.

My mother calls to say my great aunt Cecelia has died. The silence on the line is what I often imagine death to be like. Now all I can think about is a contest we had to see who could come up with a material that would protect an egg from impact. My conclusion was simple: Tupperware and Jello. The fire department was there and each kid was raised up in the truck until we could see the entire school, and the city looked like a map of a city.

Being lifted into the clouds I felt like the angels we drew under the tables during lunch that always had ropes attached to their wings. I didn't drop the egg—it was snatched from my palms by the wind, flew out over the buses and playground. I imagined it curled up and quivering in its Jell-O, as yellow as the piss in great aunt Cecelia's catheter, a little egg like a pebble of bone.

Poem for My Body

You are just a box. I knock against
you like a fly in a jar. When I am silly and crippled
you carry me like a penny in your pocket.

This is because you need me, maybe
for good luck or comfort. To have someone to talk to
when you are aching and alone. One day I will abandon you.

My name will be devoured by fog. You will rust
from the inside out, like a watch.
Time, in fact, will peel us apart,
sculpting your face with greasy fingers.
And I will be hair trimmed from the chin,
stolen by whatever can make use of what I become.

Mala #1

I liked Maria
because of how she put things together—
a dress over backwards jean, birthday cards
made of bottle caps and tape, candle wax,
and hand drawn pictures of emus. Nothing
went to waste, and when she learned
to sew she gave everyone a stuffed animal
on the last day of class. My giraffe had fins,
the head of a pink rabbit for a stomach,
felt dog tongues for ears and little beaded eyes
along its back.

It's cute, said my mother, and I agreed

until a decade later I learned how the children
at Auschwitz were separated from their parents,
how before the gas they tried dynamite
(my teacher said, *nothing went to waste*).

I read later that for months the arms and legs
that could not be reached hung in the trees,
and it is terrible, but even now I imagine Maria
threading a needle—tendon and bark—

Mala #2

When I was twelve my sister's father bought us
a pet chicken. My sister named it Food,
and we both though it was hilarious. After a year
Food was fat enough to kill, my sister's father
waking us up just as the sun peeked over the houses.

I only remember wiping my nose on my pajama sleeve,
my sister, in her surprise, mimicking the figure eight
of the headless bird.

> We used the feathers for a pillow.
> We boiled the head and the feet for flavor.

My mother mixed the meat into the salad with her bare hands.

> *Tomato. Cranberry. Walnut. Olive.*

Prayer at 3 a.m.

This is what mends you: a cup of hot water,
some milk, this hour that crouches like a vandal
in the ink, hollow between days. We were made
in a building that bends the choir of birds
to seizure, to the frosted tongue that leads.

This house does not shake. Still,
I wish the halls afire. If you are here
you know what voice I am expecting.

If it happens again I must know
why I cannot sleep, must wander,
must touch everything there is
before the sun, because we both know
what is pulled from trees,
featherless and stuffed. I know
you sent this to me

and I will make of its tone, comfort
in the city of my ears.
Where you find me, pretend

there is not violence in the windows.
The night you press into—
faith—unrolls my tongue
like a bandage upon healing.

Long Letter to the 20th Century

Sometimes I slept in your car with the back seat down and the windows open. I guess you forgot you gave me the extra key. Where I went is not important. I always had the car back by dawn. This was never out of anger. You had a cassette player and I liked to listen to Kenny G because his saxophone reminded me of my grandmother. At thirteen, I knew the theme songs to all her soap operas; pretended to be sick just to curl up on the floor at her swelling feet and avoid school, with a bag of Cheetos and a coloring book in which Musheerah had covered everything green.

My grandmother dreamed of being on *Oprah*—just to sit in the audience, for once in her life not to have to limp to the bus stop with a sharpened stick to fend off dogs.

This is how every letter should start: with a stick and a stray box of cigarettes, stray quarter for the gumball machine, stray pen to draw the house I lived in until she died. And I guess you are there, a crooked stick figure standing on the porch, waiting for me to tell you the door is unlocked so you can step into me, catch me shaving for the first time, nicking my neck, splitting the flesh like a soft tomato. Or you'll catch my shadow as it slips into the closet where I might have tried to hang myself, or the bathtub that, years later, is still running water where my baptism felt like drowning.

This was a letter to some girl, but reader we both know you better than that. You have a name, maybe a brother, maybe a favorite pillow and way you like to do your hair. Though you're thinking this is about your car or the saxophone, or the first time we kissed, and I left you with the audience of nurses at the treatment center, you're wrong. This is an apology for all I've forgotten—all the times in summer camp that I set the snakes free and said they bit me, just so I wouldn't have to kill.

You see, I recognize that my pants were a little tight in elementary school, but you were not even a stranger and I was ten. Sure, I stole my first condom and forgot to use it but that doesn't mean I deserved to have the shit kicked out of me for staying up late on a Friday to watch *Robocop*. My sister's father would never have let me write this letter.

In church I ate my grandmother's mints and convinced myself they made me invisible so god couldn't see my indifference and maybe wouldn't care that I thought he was as plastic as the mistletoe that hung over the door to the sanctuary. Even in the mouth-warm heat of July this is what I recall: David spraying aerosol over the candles, the cake and the window going up in flames like the intention behind this letter, the house across the street that burned down just months before my grandmother died, her sister at the funeral, ravaged by Alzheimer's, forgetting she was once speaking to someone she knew.

Let's pretend this is relevant—that I can still pull your name from the fog of three women in my life I have made out with and not regretted it. I gave you my name, and the rabbit's foot I carried like a knife. We burned your sister's dolls at the bon fire on the night she turned thirteen.

If I die tomorrow I won't come back for anything, not even the white snake with its jaws open wide enough to swallow this city. Yes, we T.P.'d the houses. What else was there to do in July? That summer we dressed my sister in your mother's wedding dress and the neighbors never told.

ACKNOWLEDGMENTS

I am forever grateful to the following publications in which some of these poems have appeared: *Grist:* "Our Famous Shadows"; *The Virginia Quarterly Review:* "Queen Elizabeth"; *Willow Springs:* "Moon Building."

Many thanks to Arizona State University's creative writing program and the Virginia G. Piper Center for Creative Writing for their fellowships, which allowed invaluable experience and time to write this book.

I am forever indebted to my teachers and mentors: Sally Ball, Gregory Donovan, Norman Dubie, Beckian Fritz Goldberg, Cynthia Hogue, Terry Hummer, Richard Jackson, Alberto Rios, Gary Sange, and David Wojahn. Without their encouragement and support this book would not exist.

Thanks to my friends and fellow poets for their patience and kind words: Rachel Andoga, Allysson Boggess, John-Michael Bloomquist, Christopher Emery, Christian Gerard, Spencer Hanvick, Eman Hassan, Ryan Holden, Natalia Holtzman, Darren Jackson, Shane Lake, Hugh Martin, Scott Montgomery, Catherine Murray, Fernando Pérez, Michele Poulos, and Jordan Rice.

Most importantly—thanks to my family, with limitless love.

DEXTER L. BOOTH is the 2012 winner of the Cave Canem Poetry Prize for his book *Scratching the Ghost*. He earned an MFA in creative writing from Arizona State University. His poems have appeared in *Amendment, Grist,* the *New Delta Review,* the *Virginia Quarterly Review,* and *Willow Springs.* He lives in Tempe, Arizona.

Scratching the Ghost by Dexter L. Booth is the winner of the 2012 Cave Canem Poetry Prize, selected by Major Jackson. Established in 1999, the Prize is awarded annually to an exceptional manuscript by an African American poet who has not yet published a full-length book of poems.

Support for the 2012 Prize has been provided in part by the National Endowment for the Arts and generous individual donors.

Founded in 1996 by Toi Derricotte and Cornelius Eady, Cave Canem Foundation is a home for the many voices of African American poetry and is committed to cultivating the artistic and professional growth of African American poets.

www.cavecanempoets.org

Book design by Connie Kuhnz. Composition by BookMobile Design & Digital Publisher Services, Minneapolis, Minnesota. Manufactured by Versa Press on acid-free 30 percent postconsumer wastepaper.